Colossians

Complete In Christ

#Col-NK-SS

A Bible-Based Study

For Individuals And Groups

Leader's Guide Included

Lamplighters International
Eden Prairie, Minnesota, USA 55344
www.LamplightersUSA.org

Fifth printing – October 2003

Unless otherwise noted, Scripture references are taken from the New King James Version. Copyright © 1982 by Thomas Nelson, Inc. Used by permission. All rights reserved.

Lamplighters International is a Christian discipleship ministry that publishes Bible-based, Christ-centered resources.

For additional information about the Lamplighters ministry resources contact: Lamplighters International P. O. Box 44725, Eden Prairie, Minnesota USA 55344 or visit our web site at www.LamplightersUSA.org.

ISBN # 1-931372-12-8
Order # – Col-NK-SS

Contents

How To Use This Manual

What is Lamplighters™?

Lamplighters is a Christ centered discipleship ministry that is designed to increase your understanding of God's Word and equip you to serve Him more effectively. The ministry consists of inductive Bible studies, leadership teaching materials and other resources. A Lamplighters Bible study can be completed as an individual self-study or as part of a Bible study group. Each study is a self-contained unit and an integral part of the entire Lamplighters discipleship ministry.

This Lamplighters study is comprised of five or ten individual lessons, depending on the format you choose. When you have completed the entire study you will have a much greater understanding of a significant portion of God's word. You will also have learned several new truths that you can apply to your life.

How to study a Lamplighters lesson.

A Lamplighters study begins with prayer, your Bible, the weekly lesson, and a sincere desire to learn more about God's Word. The questions are presented in a progressive sequence as you work through the study material. You should not use biblical commentaries or other biblical reference books until you have completed your weekly lesson and met with your weekly group. When you approach the Bible study in this way, you will have the opportunity to discover many valuable spiritual truths from the word of God.

As you prepare for your weekly study, find a quiet place to complete your weekly lesson. You will need approximately one hour to complete each complete lesson (Part "a" and "b". If you are new to Lamplighters, plan to spend more time on the first few lessons. Your weekly personal study time will decrease as you become familiar with the format. You will look forward each week to discovering important life principles in the coming lessons.

Each lesson is divided into two parts. While some people complete their weekly lesson at one time, others have found it beneficial to complete the studies at two different occasions. If you approach your study time in this way, you will be able to reflect more fully upon the difficult biblical passages. If you are meeting as a study group, the Group Leader or Pastor should be available to help you find the answers to any questions that are difficult for you. In addition, many people have found it helpful to begin their study early in the week so that they have enough time to meditate on the questions that require careful consideration.

Your answers should be written in your own words in the space provided on the weekly studies. We have intentionally provided a significant amount of writing space for this purpose. Write down your carefully worded and thoughtful answers with appropriate verse references unless the question calls for a personal opinion. The answers to the questions will be found in the Scripture references at the end of the questions or in the passages listed at the beginning of each study.

How To Use This Discipleship Guide.

The Lamplighters discipleship materials are designed for a variety of ministry applications. They have been used successfully in the following settings.

Self-study - Read the passage carefully that is listed at the beginning of the weekly lesson. Seek to gain as much understanding of the Text as possible. Answer the questions in the space provided using complete sentences if the space allows. Complete the entire lesson without looking at the Leader's Guide in the back of the book. Discipline yourself to answer all the questions so that you gain the maximum benefit from the lesson. When you have completed the lesson, read the corresponding portion of the Leader's Guide to gain greater understanding of the passage you have studied.

One-on-one discipleship – Complete the entire lesson without referring to the Leader's Guide. If you are leading the one-on-one discipleship meeting, become familiar with the Leader's Guide answers before you meet with the person you are discipling. Plan to meet for one hour to discuss the lesson. If you are meeting for breakfast or during the lunch hour, discipline yourself to complete the entire lesson within the scheduled time so that your meeting does not become a burden or you become a poor testimony to your employer or others. If you are not leading the study, do not look at the Leader's Guide until you have met with the person who is leading the meeting.

Small Group discipleship - The members of the discipleship group should complete their entire weekly lessons without referring to the Leader's Guide. The Group Leader should complete his or her lesson and then become thoroughly familiar with the Leader's Guide answers. A comprehensive ministry manual has been prepared for church leaders to help them how to lead small groups effectively and how to implement the Lamplighters discipleship ministry into their church ministries.

Class teaching (Adult Bible Classes) - The teacher should complete the entire lesson before class, review the Leader's Guide answers, and prayerfully consider how to present the lesson. The class members should be given the weekly lessons is advance so that they can bring their thoughtful insights and questions to the class discussion. The companion Teacher Edition with reproducible lessons is an excellent addition for those who want to use this teaching format.

"*Do you think*" Questions

Each weekly study has a few "*do you think*" questions. These questions ask you to make personal applications from the Biblical truths you are learning. Make a special effort to answer these questions because they are designed to help you apply God's Word to your life. In the first lesson the *"do you think"* questions are placed in italic print for easy identification. If you are part of a study group, your insightful answers to these questions could be a great source of spiritual encouragement to others.

Personal Questions

Occasionally you will be asked to respond to personal questions that you should do your best to answer. If you are part of a study group, you will not be asked to share any personal information about yourself. However, be sure to answer these questions for your own benefit because they will help you compare your present level of spiritual maturity to the biblical principles presented in the lesson.

A Final Word

Throughout this study, the masculine pronouns are often used in the generic sense to avoid awkward sentence construction. When the pronouns "he", "him", "his" are used to refer to the Trinity (God the father, Jesus Christ and the Holy Spirit), they always refer to the masculine gender.

This Lamplighters study is presented after many hours of careful preparation. It is our prayer that it will help you *"... grow in the grace and knowledge of our Lord and Savior Jesus Christ. To Him be the glory, both now and forever. Amen."* (2 Pet. 3:18).

_____

About the author …

John Stewart was born and raised near Winnipeg, Canada. He was drafted by the Pittsburgh Penguins (NHL) and played professional hockey for eight years. He was born again in 1977 and graduated from seminary in 1988. He served as a pastor for fifteen years and planted two Bible-believing churches. He also founded Lamplighters International where he continues to write and oversee the ministry.

Study # 1a   The Supremacy Of Christ

Read - Colossians 1:1-23; other references as given.

The ancient city of Colossae was situated about 100 miles east of Ephesus in the Roman province of Asia (now Turkey). At the time of Paul's letter to the Colossians, the church was in the process of drifting away from Christ to a form of syncretism that combined Jewish ritualism, philosophical rationalism and pagan mysticism (Note: These terms will be explained in this study). The apostle Paul wrote these timeless words of exhortation from prison " **... you are complete in Him, who is the head of all principality and power**" (Col. 2:10).

1. Paul introduced himself as ... **an apostle of Jesus Christ by the will of God** (v. 1). He included Timothy, missionary companion and spiritual brother, in his initial greeting to the church. What words does he use to describe the Colossian Christians (v. 2)?

2. The recipients of the letter are called **saints** (v. 2). When the word saint is applied to the New Testament believer it signifies God's dual calling in salvation (1 Cor. 1:2) and sanctification. Alexander Macleran, a famous Scottish preacher, said, "Saints are not an eminent sort of Christian, but all Christians are saints, and he who is not a saint is not a Christian." What are some other words the Bible uses to describe the believer's relationship to God (Jn. 1:12; Gal. 4:5, 7; 1 Pet. 2:9)?

3. Paul often expressed thankfulness for other believers (cf. Ro. 1:8; 1 Cor. 1:4; Phil. 1:3; etc.).

   a. What specific spiritual qualities was he particularly thankful for in the lives of the Colossian believers (vv. 3, 4)?

   b. In what way(s) did Paul express his gratitude for the Colossians?

    c.   In what way(s) have you recently expressed your appreciation for other Christians?

4.   The Colossian church had love for **all the saints** (v. 4). The remarkable frequency of the word **all** (twenty-eight times in only ninety-five verses) is more than coincidence - it emphasizes an important spiritual truth.

    a.   Please list the remaining phrases that include the word **all** and their corresponding verse references in chapter one.

    b.   What important spiritual truth *do you think* is being taught by the frequent use of this word?

5.   The Christian graces of faith, love, and hope form a familiar triad (trio) in Scripture (e.g., Ro. 5:2-5; 1 Cor. 13:13, 1 Thess. 1:3, 5:8). In these passages, hope is coordinated with faith and love, but here hope represents the source from which faith and love spring (vv. 4, 5). What *do you think* is meant by the phrase **...the hope which is laid up for you in heaven** (v. 5)?

6.   Paul said **... which has come to you, as it has in all the world; and is bringing forth fruit** (v. 6). To what was he referring?

7.   Most biblical scholars believe God used Epaphras to start the church at Colossae (v. 7; note: Epaphras is a shortened form of Epaphroditus but this man should not be identified with the man by the same name in Philippians 2:25 and 4:18).

    a.   Paul was obviously impressed with Epaphras's spiritual character. How did Paul describe this man (v. 7)?

    b.   Would those who know you well say the same things about your spiritual character?

8.   Paul thanked God for the Christians at Colosse (v. 3) and asked Him for a specific request on their behalf. What was it (v. 9)?

9.   Some Christians are uncertain what God wants from their lives (i.e., God's will). They appear to wander aimlessly in their Christian lives, unsure about how to please God. What four specific things does God desire all Christians to do (vv. 10b-12)?

"God said, 'Let Us make man in Our image.' Man says, 'Let us make a god according to our imagination.'"

Study # 1b   **The Supremacy Of Christ**

Read - Colossians 1:1-23; other references as given.

10. Only Christians qualify to share in a future inheritance because they have been transferred from the power or domain of darkness into the kingdom of Jesus Christ (vv. 12, 13).

    a. Several important truths regarding man's salvation are taught in verse thirteen. Please name at least three.

    b. Before an individual is saved, he is a servant of sin and a child of wrath (Ro. 6:20; Eph. 2:3). When a person trusts Christ alone for eternal life (cf. Ro. 10:9, 10, 13), he is transferred from Satan's authority to the authority of Jesus Christ (v. 13). How is the individual described after his salvation (2 Cor. 5:17, 20; Ph. 3:20)?

11. Paul begins an active assault on the theological error that had crept into the church (vv. 13 ff.). The Colossian heresy was a mixture of ritualism (i.e., religious rules without any biblical basis, e.g., legalism), philosophical rationalism (i.e., human reason that denied the reality of God, e. g. modern-day liberalism and humanism) and pagan mysticism (experience-centered religiosity, e.g., New Age, etc.). The false teachers had offered these heresies as a higher form of wisdom or enlightenment and had successfully undermined the believer's confidence about Christ's relationship to deity (v. 15a), to creation (vv. 15b-17) and to the church (v. 18).

    a. Christ is **... the image of the invisible God** (v. 15). What *do you think* this means (cf. Jn. 1:18; Heb. 1:3)?

b. In the phrase **the firstborn** (vv. 15, 18) the Greek word *prototokos* can mean first in time or first in rank. *Do you think* this statement means first in time, first in rank (supremacy), or both (vv. 16, 17)?

12. a. Give three reasons why Christ has the right to be the supreme ruler over all creation, including mankind (vv. 16, 17).

    b. Since Christ is the rightful ruler over all creation, are there still areas of your life in which you have not acknowledged Christ's lordship (e.g., life goals, sinful habits, your thoughts or attitude toward life or other people, finances, etc.)?

13. Paul said, **... in Him all things consist** (v. 17). What *do you think* this means?

14. Paul's third affirmation of Christ's supremacy over all creation includes the church. If Christ is **the head of the body, the church; who is the beginning, the firstborn from the dead; that in all things he might have the preeminence** (v. 18). What practical implications *do you think* this spiritual truth should have upon a local church ministry?

15. The Colossian heretics taught that truth was a subjective enlightenment, but the Word of God teaches that truth comes objectively through a person, Jesus Christ (note: there are 17 references to Christ in vv. 15-20 that emphasize this truth, cf. **in Him, through Him, by Him,** etc.). What *do you think* is meant by the statement **it pleased the Father that in Him all the fullness should dwell** (v. 19)?

16. a. Man is not rescued from the domain of darkness by intellectual enlightenment but by Jesus Christ, the Redeemer of men (vv. 13, 14). How is man, who is alienated from God and hostile toward God, actually delivered or saved from his desperate situation (vv. 20-23; Jn. 3:36)?

   b. Have you been saved or born again according to God's holy Word? When and where did that happen?

Psalm 119:105   "Your word is a lamp to my feet and a light to my path."

Study # 2a   **The Treasures Of Christ**

Christ is not an abstract principle that elevates man to a new level of spiritual enlightenment, but a Person who gave His blood on the cross to reconcile all things to Himself (v. 20). His authority extends over all creation from the highest heavens to the highest courts of human judgment. In this lesson, the apostle Paul explains how the lordship of Christ should affect the Christian's life.

1. In what way(s) did Paul demonstrate Christ's authority over his life (v. 24; cf. 2 Tim. 1:8)?

2. Many Christians rejoice when God blesses their lives, but they find it difficult to praise Him during the trials of life. Paul was able to rejoice during his sufferings as a prisoner (v. 24).

    a. Paul knew two important spiritual truths that helped him to rejoice in his sufferings rather than grumble or complain about his situation. What are they (Col. 1:16-18)?

    b. Think of a negative situation in your life over which you have little or no control (e.g., family or work problem, etc.). What do you think you can do to bring more glory to God during this trial?

3. Although many believers would not consider prison an effective place for ministry, Paul continued to serve God faithfully (v. 24; **... fill up in my flesh what is lacking of the afflictions of Christ for the sake of His body)**. List five things Paul did to serve the Lord in prison (Col. 1:1-3, 9; Acts 16:25, 28-32; 2 Tim. 4:13).

4. The difficult phrase **... fill up in my flesh what is lacking of the afflictions of Christ** ... has been the topic of much debate (v. 24). Many Roman Catholics interpret the "afflictions" of Christ as Christ's redemptive sufferings on the cross. They believe that followers of Christ must also suffer to complete the work of redemption.

    a. How can we be sure that this verse does not teach this theological perspective (Col. 2:12, 13; Jn. 19:30; Heb. 10:10-12)?

    b. If the phrase **...... fill up that is lacking of the afflictions of Christ** does not refer to salvation, what *do you think* it means?

5. Paul was commissioned by God to be a minister (Gr. *diakonos* - minister, servant, deacon) to the church (v. 25). His responsibility was to equip God's people by preaching the word of God (v. 25).

    a. What phrase does Paul use to prove that he fully accepted Christ's supremacy and authority over this aspect of his life (v. 25)?

    b. Paul verbally acknowledged Christ's authority over his life to an entire church (v. 25). Have you acknowledged Christ's supremacy and authority over your life (your work, goals, family, etc.) to God?   If you haven't, why not bow before God in prayer and acknowledge Jesus Christ's authority over every aspect of your life?

6. The Colossian heretics taught that a mystery was a secret teaching known only to an exclusive group and unknown to the masses. Only those who were initiated by certain "anointed" leaders could become enlightened by the truth.

    a.   What did Paul say to the Corinthian believers who were also being tempted by false teachers (2 Cor. 11:2, 3)?

    b.   What did Paul say to the Galatian believers who were being led astray by false teachers (Gal. 3:3)?

7.   The Colossian church was being deceived by false religious leaders who claimed to possess a special anointing from God and promised their followers spiritual enlightenment. Even today the church of Jesus Christ continues to fall prey to spiritual entrapment. Why do you think Christians are so easily led astray by false teachers?

8.   The real **mystery** (Gr. *mysterion* - mystery, secret; used in the New Testament of truth undiscoverable except through divine revelation, cf. 1 Cor. 2:6-10) of God is available to all who will come to Christ in faith (v. 26, "saints"). If the mystery of God is not some secret spiritual enlightenment, what is the mystery that God has revealed to His people?

"Christ's faithful servants are to follow His example, to quarrel with error, to fight against sin, to be aggressive against everything that is opposed to our Lord and His truth."

Charles Haddon Spurgeon

Study # 2b   The Treasures Of Christ

9. In contrast to the covert or secretive methods of the false teachers, Paul and his followers proclaimed (Gr. *kataggello* - declare, proclaim publicly, publish) the message of Christ to everyone who would listen (v. 28).

    a. What was their objective (v. 28)?

    b. What did they do to accomplish their goal (vv. 28, 29)?

    c. Do you strive to see others come to Christ and understand the riches of His glory?

10. The lordship of Christ led Paul to suffer as a prisoner (Col. 4:10, 18) and to work tirelessly for the salvation of others (Col. 1:28, 29). A third aspect of Paul's ministry was his constant concern for all the churches (Col. 2:1; 2 Cor. 11:28). What do you think was the conflict he experienced on behalf of the churches at Colossae and Laodicea and other believers whom he had never met (v. 1)?

11. What thing(s) did Paul want to see accomplished in their lives (v. 2)?

12. Some Christians believe that consistent fellowship in a church is an option to be considered rather than a command to be obeyed (cf. Heb. 10:24, 25). Their inconsistency in attendance can make them largely ineffective in ministry, a stumbling block to new believers, and unaware of the needs of other believers. There is yet another negative result of not being a bonded member of a local church (v. 2; **... being knit together in love**). What is it (v. 2)?

13. The Colossian heretics taught that divine truth was acquired through their spiritual instruction. Like many false teachers today, their followers became addicted to their ministries.

    a. Where should all Christians go to find the knowledge of God (vv. 2, 3)?

    b. Why should Colossian believers and all Christians seek Him (Christ) only?

14. Unfortunately, some Christians do not seek Christ with all their hearts. What are some things you think Christians can do in an attempt to find the knowledge of God?

15. What words would you use to describe Paul's pursuit of God as revealed in the person of Jesus Christ (Phil. 3:7-14)?

16. In another New Testament letter, Paul said that some men were **... always learning and never able to come to the knowledge of the truth** (2 Tim. 3:7). It has been said that "atheism denies truth, agnosticism doubts truth, rationalism questions truth, hedonism mocks truth and education gropes for truth."

    a. What did Jesus say about truth (Jn. 14:6, 17:17)?

    b.   If you are a Christian, are you absolutely convinced that Jesus Christ is the embodiment of truth and that the Bible is the infallible Word of God?

17.   Even though many Christians know that the source of all wisdom and knowledge is Jesus Christ, they struggle to make Christ a living reality in their lives. They see Christ as a hard taskmaster who is always ready to give them an endless list of spiritual responsibilities.

    a.   In the statement **... as you therefore have received Christ Jesus the Lord, so walk in Him** (v. 6), there are at least two important spiritual truths that will help every believer in his relationship with Christ. What are they (v. 6; cf. Jn. 15:5)?

    b.   Paul's frequent use of the word **walk** (Col. 1:10; 2:6; Gr. *peripateo* - to walk, to conduct one's life in a certain way) suggests a continuous manner of living. Besides the answers you gave in part "a" of this question, how can a Christian fulfill this command (v. 7)?

Psalm 119:105 "Your word is a lamp to my feet and a light to my path."

Study # 3a **The Fullness Of Christ**

Read - Colossians 2:8-23; other references as given.

Christ's supremacy extends over all creation (Co. 1:14-20) and should lead every believer to a life of dedicated Christian service (1:21-2:7). In this study, the apostle Paul identifies the four errors of the Colossian heretics that threaten to draw Christians away from their devotion to Christ: false philosophy (2:8-10), legalism (2:11-17), mysticism (2:18, 19) and asceticism (2:20-23).

1. The first error taught by the false teachers at Colossae was false philosophy (v. 8). The word **philosophy** (Gr. *philosophia* - love of wisdom) can be used either positively (a love of the wisdom of God) or negatively (a love for the wisdom of man, cf. 1 Cor. 1:20-25; Ja. 3:13-16).

    a. Give three characteristics of false philosophy or empty deception that make it particularly dangerous to the church (v. 8).

    b. What were the Colossian believers to protect themselves against (v. 8)?

2. How were the Colossians to protect themselves against this spiritual danger (v. 8)?

3. In other New Testament letters, Paul uses military terminology to describe the battle that believers must wage in order to be victorious over false reasonings (Eph. 6:10-17; 2 Cor. 10:3-5).

a.   Why should God's people reject all philosophies (the wisdom of men) that contradict the Word of God (1 Cor. 1:20-25; Ja. 3:13-16)?

b.   What did Paul do when he found that false philosophies had crept into his own thinking (2 Cor. 10:4, 5)?

4.   The philosophies of this world are empty and hollow because they are based upon the false teachings of fallen men who do not understand the fear of the Lord, which is the beginning of wisdom (Pro. 9, 10). With what is the emptiness of these philosophies compared (v. 9)?

5.   Paul contrasts the insufficiency of humanistic philosophy with the sufficiency of Christ (vv. 8-10). What do you think is meant by the phrase **... and you are complete in Him** (v. 10)?

6.   The second heresy that threatened the Colossian church was legalism (vv. 11-17). The abrupt and unexpected reference to circumcision suggests that Paul is replying to the claim made by the false teachers for its necessity (v. 11). To accept circumcision as an adult on religious grounds meant that the believer was placing himself under the authority of the Old Testament Mosaic Law.

a.   Is a Christian under the Old Testament Mosaic Law (i.e., the Law of God given to Moses at Mt. Sinai; Ro. 6:14, 10:4; Gal. 3:19-25)?   Why?

b.   How did Paul and Barnabas respond to the men who came from Jerusalem and insisted that the believers at Antioch had to be circumcised (Acts 15:1, 2)?

    c.   Is it possible for an individual to be truly born again and yet be unsure about his continuing relationship to the Law of Moses (Acts 15:4-7)?

7.   What did Paul teach the Colossian Christians regarding their need for circumcision (Col. 2:11)?

8.   Some Christians continue to be plagued with doubts about their relationship with Christ. This lack of assurance robs them of the joy that Christ wants them to experience and greatly hinders their effectiveness in His service.

    a.   What does the Bible say about Christ's work of redemption that should bring joy and assurance to the heart of every believer (vv. 13-15)?

    b.   Has Christ canceled your **... handwriting of requirements that was against us**? Have you trusted Christ alone for everlasting life or are you trusting in something else (baptism, confirmation, good works, church membership, etc.) to save you (cf. Ro. 10:9, 10, 13)?

"If you wish to be disappointed, look to others. If you wish to be downhearted, look to yourself. If you wish to be encouraged... look to Christ."
Eric Sauer

Study # 3b   **The Fullness Of Christ**

Read - Colossians 2:8-23; other references as given.

9. Legalism is a tyrannical ruler that places increasingly heavy demands upon its subjects.

   a. Why do you think some believers are so willing to place themselves under a form of legalistic Christianity?

   b. Are there religious beliefs that you previously held but have come to realize that they were nothing more than the traditions of men?
   Please give an example, if you can.

10. a. What did Paul say to the Colossian believers regarding the observance of the Old Testament dietary regulations and religious festivals (v. 16)?

    b. The phrase **... let no one therefore judge you ...** is interesting because no Christian can control the thoughts of another Christian. What do you think a Christian should do to fulfill this biblical command (cf. Gal. 5:1)?

c. How does Paul describe the various aspects of the Old Testament Mosaic Law (feasts, regulations, sacrifices, etc.; v. 17; Heb. 8:5, 10:1)? As a shadow of what or who (Col. 2:17)?

11. Do you make observance of Old Testament laws (dietary, ceremonial, etc.) or your own personal convictions a test of fellowship of spirituality with other believers?

12. Describe the third doctrinal error that the Colossian believers were to guard against (vv. 18, 19).

13. Mysticism is the belief that direct knowledge of God, spiritual truth, or ultimate reality can be obtained through subjective experience rather than the Word of God. Unfortunately, it continues to be a threat to the church today because it appeals to the fleshly nature of immature Christians who want to experience the presence of God but do not want to commit themselves to a diligent study of the Word (cf. Jn. 8:31, 32; 17:17; Ro. 10:17).

a. While mysticism promises a closer relationship with God, it actually draws people away from Christ (v. 19; i.e., the Head, cf. 1:18). What is another negative result of this doctrinal deviation (v. 19)?

b. What are some examples of modern religious mysticism?

14. The Colossian heretics taught a fourth theological error - asceticism (pronounced a-set-e-siz-em). Asceticism is the practice of strict self-denial as a measure of personal and spiritual discipline. Throughout the centuries, various religious groups have adopted difficult and even painful restrictions (cf. severe treatment of the body, v. 23) as a means of gaining control over the sinful desires of the body.

   a. Why does religious asceticism appear to be a legitimate method of controlling the fleshly desires of the sin nature (v. 23).

   b. What did Paul say about the effectiveness of this method of spiritual growth (v. 23)?

15. It is possible that the study of these four doctrinal errors has caused you to think seriously about your relationship with Christ and your spiritual advancement. Take a moment to honestly evaluate the four errors discussed in this study (human philosophy, legalism, mysticism, and asceticism). Is there one of these four errors that you find easy to accept as truth?   Why?

16. What spiritual advice would you give another Christian who has allowed himself to adopt one of these four heresies?

Psalm 119:105 "Your word is a lamp to my feet and a light to my path."

Study # 4a The Renewal From Christ

Read - Colossians 3:1-17; other references as given.

When people say that an individual is "so heavenly minded that he is no earthly good," they are saying the person's spiritual devotion to God has little or no practical benefit to the world around him. However, if God's people are not heavenly minded (in a right way), they are no earthly good (as God's ambassadors). In the final two chapters, the doctrine of Christ's supremacy is applied to the various aspects of the believer's life.

1. The great doctrines of the Bible (e.g., Christ's supremacy, God's sovereignty, man's depravity and redemption, the resurrection, etc.) are not simply intellectual puzzles for the spiritually inclined. They are the foundation for all that the believer is or ever will be in Christ. (Note: the word **then**, v. 1; Gr. *oun* - therefore, then; indicates that the supremacy of Christ is the motive behind the exhortations for godly living.)

    a. If a person has been saved (been raised with Christ), what should he be doing (v. 1)?

    b. What do you think a Christian can do to fulfill the command to seek **... those things which are above** (v. 1)?

2. The commands to **... seek those things which are above** (v. 1) and **... set your mind on things above** (v. 2) are similar, yet distinct. What do you think is the difference between these two commands?

3. The believer is supposed to **... set your mind on things above, not on things on the earth** (v. 2). How can a Christian fulfill this command in a physical world that requires his constant administration?

4. When some Christians give their personal testimony, they say that Christ died for them. However, there is another significant event that took place at the time of their salvation. What is it (v. 3)?

5. Paul spoke forthrightly about the demands of the resurrected life and the Christian's need to claim victory over the passions of the flesh (v. 5 ff.). One biblical commentator said, "The old life is dead; let it die."

    a. List the specific sins over which Christ has given every Christian victory (v. 5).

    b. The phrase **... lived in them** (v. 7) refers to the time prior to salvation when an individual's life was dominated by a desire to fulfill the evil practices mentioned in verse five. If you are a Christian, do you have consistent victory over these specific areas?

    c. To what is the sin of **covetousness** compared (v. 5)?

6. The first catalog of sins addresses the Christian's need to remove himself from the sins of the flesh (v. 5). The second list focuses attention on the sins of the believer's attitude and speech (v. 8).

    a. What word does Paul use to emphasize when a Christian should rid himself of these sins (v. 8)?

    b. The imagery of the phrase **put off all these** (Gr. *apotithemi* - to lay aside, to put off) is that of putting off clothes - like stripping off soiled and filthy garments. Instead of putting off filthy garments, what sins are Christians to put off (vv. 8, 9)?

7.   At first glance, the terms **anger, wrath** and **malice** appear to be synonyms (v. 8). However, there are important differences between these terms.

   a.   Please give a definition of each term (anger, wrath, malice), being careful to show the important difference between them. (Note: you may use a dictionary if you wish.)

   b.   Have you laid aside the evil practices of slandering others and abusive speech?

8.   Many of God's people struggle in their relationship with Christ because they have never understood the biblical basis for victorious Christian living - union with Christ. They are busy "doing Christianity" rather than allowing Christ to live through them (cf. Jn. 15:5). Their lives are often marked by guilt, a judgmental or critical spirit, and a preoccupation with negative motivation (e.g., "You can't do that."; "I shouldn't do that."; "A good Christian would never do that.").

   a.   If a Christian understands his union with Christ and sincerely desires to seek the things above, he will naturally put off those things that are not pleasing to Christ (vv. 5-9). What else should he do (v. 10)?

   b.   The replacement principle (putting off and putting on) is an important spiritual concept. The phrase **... put on the new man ...** cannot refer to salvation because it would make man the author of his own redemption. What do you think this phrase means (v. 10)?

"When I first went to China I asked God to help me with my work. After I was there for a while, I prayed that I would be able to help God with His work. Finally, I asked God to do His work through me."

Hudson Taylor

Study # 4b   **The Renewal From Christ**

Read - Colossians 3:1-17; other references as given.

9. The spiritual rebirth that Christ offers mankind has profound implications. Man, once enslaved to sin and mired in an earthly existence without meaning or hope, is rescued by the King of kings. The believer is given a new perspective on life (vv. 1-4), a new power over sin (vv. 5-9) and a new priority - to love others (v. 10 ff.). What will happen when God's people are **... renewed in knowledge according to the image of Him who created him** (vv. 10, 11; cf. Gal. 3:28)?

10. Can you honestly say that Christ has enabled you to regard all men equally, regardless of the color of their skin, their cultural background, or their economic status in life?

11. Paul instructs the Colossian believers to adopt certain Christian virtues that would reflect their new nature (v. 12; elect of God, holy, beloved). Their willingness to live in harmony is a glory to God but makes them an enigma to the world (cf. Jn. 13:34, 35; 17:21-23). For this diverse family to live in harmony with each other, Christians must clothe themselves with **... tender mercies, kindness, humility, meekness, longsuffering** (v. 12).

    a. Mercy (Gr. *oiktirmos*) is a Christian virtue that causes the believer to be moved with feelings of tenderness while he attempts to relieve the sufferings and needs of others. In what way(s) do the sufferings and needs of others consistently move you emotionally and cause you to help relieve their distress?

    b. Kindness (Gr. *chrestotes*) combines the qualities of goodness, kindliness and graciousness. It might be defined as "sweetness of disposition." Does this describe your general disposition as you conduct the routine affairs of daily living?

c.   Humility (Gr. *tapeinophrosne*) and meekness (Gr. *prautes*) are spiritual characteristics that are essential for harmonious relations with others. Longsuffering (Gr. *makroththumia*) denotes the self-restraint that enables a believer to bear insult or injury without resorting to retaliation. How can a Christian manifest these three qualities when he feels threatened or attacked (e.g., at work, at home, at church)?

12.   The word **bearing** (v. 12) defines the believer's goal of putting up with minor irritations and imperfections of others. Are you more tolerant or less tolerant of the faults of other people in your life than you were a year ago?

13.   Even though God's people can be very diligent about incorporating these qualities into their lives, they will still fall short of fulfilling His plan if they do not allow charity to motivate their actions (v. 14; cf. 1 Cor. 13:1-13). Besides love (charity), what else should a Christian do to fulfill God's plan for his life (vv. 15-17)?

14.   Many Christians understand their relationship with God to be purely vertical. While concentrating on their heavenly union with Christ, they forget that He had placed them into a family (the church) on earth. List the phrases that specifically identify the believer's responsibility to other members of the body of Christ (vv. 9-17; e.g., **Do not lie to one another,** v. 9.).

Psalm 119:105 "Your word is a lamp to my feet and a light to my path."

Study # 5a   The New Self In Christ

Read - Colossians 3:18-4:18; other references as given.

Like several other New Testament letters, the book of Colossians moves progressively from the believer's relationship with Christ to his responsibilities to Christ. The doctrine of Christ's supremacy is not a bare theological fact but a life-changing principle that should affect every aspect of the believer's life. In this final study, Paul offers specific instruction as to how God's people can manifest the supremacy of Christ in their lives.

1. a.   How can a married woman acknowledge the supremacy of Christ in her life?

    b.   What two things can a married man do to acknowledge the supremacy of Christ in his life?

    c.   How can children acknowledge the supremacy of Christ in their lives?

2.   Some Christians reject the biblical teaching of female submission within the marriage bond. They believe that Christ's death eliminated all social and gender distinctions (cf. Gal. 3:28) and the biblical passages that promote the wife's submission are culturally obsolete. While Christ's death does provide every person equal access to God, it did not obliterate the social order.

    a.   Give at least two reasons why the biblical teaching regarding the wife's submission to her husband should not be ignored (v. 18; 1 Cor. 11:12).

    b.   There are at least three truths taught in verse eighteen about the wife's submission in marriage. Please list them.

3.   Many professional marriage counselors emphasize the individual partner's rights within the marriage bond (e.g., the right to be happy, the right to self-expression, etc.). What does the Bible emphasize in the marriage relationship (Col. 3:18, 19; Eph. 5:22-33)?

4.   A father can greatly influence his children for Christ if he assumes his God-given responsibility as spiritual leader of the home. On the other hand, he can be a major reason why his children rebel against God. He can provoke his children to **wrath** (Eph. 6:4) and even exasperate them to the point that they become discouraged (Col. 3:21). What do you think a Christian father should do to avoid these devastating parental errors?

5.   Having completed his instruction on the family, Paul now addresses the relationship between the servant and his master (Col. 3:22-4:1). The ancient servant was to demonstrate his willingness to acknowledge the supremacy of Christ by submitting to his master (v. 22).

    a.   List the specific ways that describe the particular manner in which the slave's obedience was to be fulfilled (vv. 22, 23)?

    b.   Do you think it is right to apply the biblical teaching regarding the servant-master relationship in the modern employee-employer relationship? Why?

6.   Sometimes Christians can become embittered against their employers because they feel overworked or under appreciated. When this happens, they are tempted to work in a manner that is not pleasing to God and their employers. Paul states an important truth that will help a Christian maintain a proper attitude toward his employer. What is it (vv. 22-24)? Note: it is stated twice, but in different words.

7.   Unfortunately, some Christians are poor workers and even disrespectful of their employers. They steal from their employers by coming in late, leaving early and not doing their work heartily as an ambassador for God. What stern warning does the Bible give Christians who will not fulfill their responsibilities in the workplace (v. 25)?

8.   Christian employers are supposed to treat their employees with justice and fairness. With all the pressure on corporate profitability, how can a Christian employer consistently fulfill this biblical command (Col. 4:1)?

"God continues to present a supreme order to life. Man constantly pursues a selfish agenda. Who shall win in the end?"

Study # 5b   **The New Self In Christ**

9. Believers are supposed to **continue earnestly in prayer, being vigilant in it with thanksgiving** (v. 2). What do you think this means?

10. On several occasions, Paul asked the churches to pray for him (cf. Eph. 6:19; 1 Thess. 5:25; 2 Thess. 3:1).

    a.   What did Paul ask the Colossian believers to pray on his behalf (vv. 3, 4)?

    b.   Do you often ask other believers to pray for you?

11. What do you think it means to **walk in wisdom toward those who are outside** (v. 5)?

12. Many biblical scholars believe that the original concerns about the ministry (i.e., the Colossian heresy) were brought to Paul by Epaphras (cf. Col. 1:7, 8). Paul's letter to the Colossians was subsequently hand delivered by Tychicus and Onesimus (Col. 4:7-9). How does Paul describe these two Christian servants?

13. The New Testament is filled with lesser known saints of God who were greatly used as servants of Christ. Their willingness to acknowledge the supremacy of Christ led some of them to martyrdom (cf. Acts 7:59, 60; 12:1, 2), others to prison (cf. Acts 16:23) and still others to risk their lives for the work of Christ. Name three lesser-known Christian servants who risked their lives for the work of God (Ro. 16:3, 4; Phil. 2:25-30).

14. At the time of Paul's letter to the Colossians, it appears that Epaphras was not planning to return to the church. Apparently the spiritual oversight of the church had been assumed by Archippus (v. 17).

    a. How did Epaphras continue to minister to the believers at Colossae and the other churches of the Lycus Valley (Laodicea, Hierapolis) after his departure (vv. 12, 13)?

    b. Paul's letter was originally sent to the saints and faithful brethren at Colossae (Col. 1:2). What did Paul want them to tell Archippus (v. 17)?

    c. What was Paul's final request from the believers at Colossae?

15. Summarize the central theme or message of the book of Colossians in one complete sentence.

16. Name the four heretical teachings that had found their way into the Colossian church.

17. What were the most significant spiritual truths taught in this study of the book of Colossians.

Congratulations:

You have just completed a challenging study of a very special book of the Bible. If you have completed all five studies you will likely have a better understanding of the supremacy of Christ "for it pleased the Father that in him should all fullness dwell (Col. 1:19) for in Him dwelleth all the fullness of the Godhead bodily..." (Col. 2:9). Brethren, reject the emptiness of human philosophies, the bondage of legalism, the subjectivity and confusion of mysticism, and the misplaced confidence of asceticism. Seek those things which are above, where Christ sitteth on the right hand of God (Col. 3:1), knowing that of the Lord you shall receive the reward of the inheritance (Col. 3:24). Grace be with you (Col. 4:18).

Psalm 119:105 "Your word is a lamp to my feet and a light to my path."

Study # 1   The Supremacy of Christ

1. Saints and faithful brethren (brothers) in Christ.

2. 1. "Children of God" (Jn. 1:12). 2. "Sons" (Gal. 4:5). 3. "Heirs" (Gal. 4:7). 4. "A chosen generation" (1 Pet. 2:9). 5. "A royal priesthood" (1 Pet. 2:9). 6. "A holy nation" (1 Pet. 2:9). 7. "His own special people" (1 Pet. 2:9).

3. a. He was thankful for their faith in Christ and their love for other Christians.
   b. 1. He prayed for them regularly (v. 3).
       2. He told them he was grateful for the letter.
   c. Answers will vary.

4. a. 1. All the world (v. 6). 2. All wisdom (v. 9). 3. All might (v. 11). 4. All patience (v. 11). 5. All things (v. 16). 6. All things (v. 17). 7. All things (v. 17). 8. All things (v. 18). 9. All the fullness (v. 19). 10. All things (v. 20). 11. All wisdom (v. 28).
   b. The remarkable frequency of the word "all" is evidently directed toward the universality of the plan of God in this world. It is also a refutation of the Colossian errorists' claim of secret special enlightenment that trapped their naive followers into an addictive spiritual bondage. There is a powerful spiritual lesson here for believers of all ages. God's truth is universal and He will give spiritual understanding to all who come to Him in faith.

5. Hope is viewed as a treasure that is being accumulated in heaven. This hope is credited to a specific account (for you) and the place of the deposit is heaven. It is interesting to notice that a clear perspective on eternity (the believer's hope) affects the present. Thus the future can be said to determine the present, for what is reserved in heaven for the believer now exercises a decisive influence upon his present conduct.

6. The Word of truth that is the gospel (v. 5).

7. a. As a dear fellowservant and a faithful servant of Christ.
   b. Answers will vary.

8. He prayed that they would be filled with the knowledge of God's will in all spiritual wisdom and understanding.

9. 1. They should bear fruit in everything they do (v. 10).
    2. They should learn God's Word (v. 10).
    3. They should allow God's grace to strengthen them for every spiritual task (v. 11).
    4. They should conduct their various duties in life with an attitude of grateful praise to God the Father (v. 12).

10. a. 1. It is God who delivers man from the domain of darkness. Man does not rescue himself.
        2. God's deliverance is a finished act, "He delivered us."
        3. Man can experience the assurance of this deliverance. Paul spoke with assurance of his personal deliverance.
        4. Man is either living in the domain of darkness or in the kingdom of Jesus Christ. There is no other option or place.
        5. Certain other answers could apply.
    b. 1. A new creation (2 Cor. 5:17).
        2. An ambassador (2 Cor. 5:20).
        3. A citizen of heaven (Ph. 3:20).

11. a. The Greek word for image (*eikon*, cf. icon - image) expresses two ideas. Christ is the likeness or image of God the Father in the sense that He is the exact likeness of Him, like the reflection of one in a mirror (Heb. 1:3). The second idea in the word is manifestation. Jesus Christ is the image of God the Father in the sense that He reveals the nature and being of God (Jn. 1:18). Paul's statement leaves no room for the Colossian heretic's vague concept of the partial deity who was becoming progressively more and more God (cf. modern-day Mormonism, New Age, etc.).
    b. Both. The primary meaning appears to be first in rank. The term firstborn does not refer to temporary priority but to Christ's unique supremacy over all creation. As all things were created by Him and for Him (v. 16), He stands over His creation as both Lord and Master.

12. a. 1. All things were created through Him (v. 16).
        2. All things were created for Him (v. 16).
        3. In Him all things consist (v. 17).
    b. Answers will vary.

13. Christ is both the unifying principle and the personal sustainer of all creation. The unity of the creation derives its cohesiveness and continuance from its creator, Jesus Christ. He is, as one biblical scholar said, "the principle of cohesion makes the universe "a cosmos instead of a chaos.""

14. In a local church every aspect of the ministry must acknowledge the supremacy of Christ and willingly submit to His headship and authority. There should be a repudiation of all attempts to build a kingdom of man that brings glory to men but fails to acknowledge the will of God and the authority of His Word. The effectiveness of church ministries should not be evaluated by human standards but by their adherence to the lordship of Christ. This does not mean that new methods of ministry should not be tried. They are acceptable as long as they adhere to the principles of God's Word.

15. It was God the Father's pleasure and will for all the sum and substance of divine entitlement to dwell in Christ. Christ was not partially God or becoming God - He was and is the very embodiment of all that was and ever will be God. The great biblical scholar John Calvin understood the word "fullness" (Gr. *pleroma*) to mean, "fullness of righteousness, wisdom, power, and every blessing", explaining that "whatever God has, He has conferred upon His Son." This statement confronted the Colossian heretic's idea that supernatural beings (Christ included) were in the process of becoming God. The word dwell (Gr. *kaoikesai*) emphasizes the permanent residence of the fullness of Christ's deity.

16. a. Man is delivered from the domain of darkness and transferred to the kingdom of Jesus Christ by a sovereign act of a loving God who died on a cross (vv. 13, 20). Christ's death on the cross removed the enmity between God and man (God's wrath, cf. Jn. 3:36) and brings peace (the absence of hostility) to all those who exercise sincere faith in Christ's redemptive act (v. 23). Those who trust in Christ alone for eternal life are now reconciled to God and are holy and blameless and beyond reproach in His sight (i.e., positional sanctification).
    b. Answers will vary.

Study # 2   **The Treasures Of Christ**

1. 1. He willingly suffered for the cause of Christ.
   2. He maintained a biblical attitude (rejoiced) in the face of adversity.

2. a. 1. Paul understood the sovereignty of God (v. 16). This allowed him to accept the things that God allowed to come into his life as His providential plan.
      2. Paul accepted God's authority over all aspects of his life including his attitude (v. 18, "that in all things he might have the preeminence"). Because he was able to see his present situation (imprisonment) as a part of God's plan, he was able to accept it as an opportunity for service rather than viewing his situation as human misfortune.
   b. Answers will vary.

3. 1. He wrote letters of instruction and encouragement to the other believers (Col. 1:1-3).
    2. He prayed for other believers (Col. 1:9).
    3. He praised God in the midst of difficult circumstances (Acts 16:25).
    4. He witnessed to others of the saving power of Jesus Christ (Acts 16:28-32).
    5. He continued to study the Word of God (2 Tim. 4:13).

4. a. 1. The book of Colossians teaches that Jesus has forgiven us of our transgressions (Col. 2:12, 13).
        2. The gospel of John teaches that the work of redemption is finished (Jn. 19:30).
        3. The book of Hebrews teaches that Jesus offered one sacrifice for sins for all time (Heb. 10:10-12).
    b. The Greek word for afflictions (*thlipsis*) is never used in the New Testament for Christ's sufferings on the cross. The word means distress, pressure or trouble, which Paul experienced in generous supply (cf. 2 Cor 11:23-29). What Paul is saying is Christ's relationship with His church is so intimate (Christ is the head and we are the body) that He continues to suffer vicariously when His followers are persecuted. Christ asked Saul on the road to Damascus, "why are you persecuting me?" (Acts 26:14), an obvious reference to His vicarious suffering, since He was in heaven. Paul was saying that he was willing to do his part for the work of Christ.

5. a. "Stewardship from God."
    b. Answers will vary.

6. a. He said he was jealous for them because he wanted to present them to Christ as a pure virgin (i.e., he wanted them to stay spiritually undefiled). He said he was fearful that they were being led astray from the simplicity and purity of Jesus Christ.
    b. "Are you so foolish? Having begun in the Spirit, are you now being made perfect by the flesh?" Since the Galatian believers had been saved through the regenerating work of the Holy Spirit (cf. Titus 3:5; "renewing of the Holy Spirit") there was no way that they were going to become spiritually mature by resorting to the man-made doctrines of Jewish ritualism.

7. 1. Many Christians do not have a strong biblical foundation so they become easy targets for those who are masters at spiritual manipulation.
    2. Many Christians have never analyzed the source of the foundation of the Christian faith. They are not sure if divine authority lies in the Word, the words of religious leaders, or of spiritual experience.
    3. Many Christians seem satisfied to allow someone else to simply tell them what the Bible says rather than studying it themselves.
    4. Other answers could apply.

8. "Christ in you, the hope of glory" (v. 27, cf. 2:2).

9. a. Their objective was to present every man perfect (spiritually mature in Jesus Christ.
    b. 1. They preached the message of Christ through individual instruction (i.e., warning every man) and teaching (v. 28).
        2. They worked tirelessly (v. 29, "I also labor").
        3. They relied on the Lord's strength rather than their human abilities (v. 29).
    c. Answers will vary.

10. The struggle or conflict was likely Paul's diligent prayer on behalf of those he had not met and had only received scant information about their spiritual well-being.

11. 1   He wanted their hearts to be knit together in love.
    2. He wanted them to come to a point of spiritual maturity, i.e., the full assurance of the knowledge of Christ.

12. If a Christian does not participate in regular fellowship with other believers, he will not experience their love that will help him grow in his faith in Christ. The spiritual encouragement that a Christian experiences from other believers is not only a source of comfort but is also the seedbed of spiritual growth.

13. a. Jesus Christ.
    b. A Christian should seek Him because in Him are hidden all the treasures of wisdom and knowledge.

14. 1. Some seek religious experience. 2. Some seek acceptance from a particular religious group or denomination. 3. Some seek spiritual knowledge that only leads to pride and arrogance (cf. 1 Cor. 8:1). 4. Some seek the teachings of religious leaders in an attempt to find the knowledge of God. 5. Some seek an eclectic concept of wisdom by borrowing a little from the Word of God and other sources (cf. 1 Cor. 1:12 ff.). Other answers could apply.

15. 1. Single-minded. 2. Passionate. 3. Diligent. 4. Several other answers could apply.

16. a. 1. "I am ... the truth..." 2. "Your word is truth."
    b. Answers will vary.

17. a. 1. The word "as" indicates a comparison. Individuals come to Christ in total humility and they should continue to live their Christian lives in humble submission to Him.
        2. The word "walk" indicates that the Christian life is not the fulfillment of a series of Christian duties, but a manner of living in which the believer communes with God as he conducts the affairs of everyday life.

b.   The believer needs to become firmly established in the faith and growing in his relationship with Christ. He needs to allow the grace of God to flood his heart and life with praise so that he can become a living testimonial of gratitude for what God has done and is doing in his life.

Study # 3   **The Fullness Of Christ**

1. a. 1. It is according to the traditions of men (i.e., it is humanistic).
          2. It is according to the basic (ungodly) principles of this world.
          3. It is not in accordance with the teachings of Christ.
    b. The Colossian believers were to guard against being lead astray by false teachings which included humanistic philosophy and anything else that was contrary to the teachings of Christ.

2.   They were not to allow any teacher to spoil them (i.e., to deceive them into believing philosophies contrary to the truth they had been taught). The Colossian believers were to guard against being lead astray by false teachings that included humanistic philosophy and anything else that was contrary to the teachings of Christ.

3. a. 1. They are unable to bring an individual to the knowledge of God (1 Cor. 1:21).
          2. They are inferior to the wisdom of God (1 Cor. 1:25).
          3. They only lead to strife and disharmony (Ja. 3:13-16).
    b. He allowed his thoughts to be confronted with the truth of God's Word.
When his thoughts contradicted the Word of God, he must deliberately choose to relinquish his own ideas and accept the teachings of the Word of God.
Paul's use of the phrase "spoil you" indicates that he regarded his own thoughts as enemies if they conflicted with the Word of God. He zealously eliminated all thoughts from his mind that were opposed to the truth ("every high thing, every thought").

4.   The emptiness of humanistic philosophies are contrasted with the fullness of Jesus Christ.

5.   The believer has all that he spiritually needs and wants in Jesus Christ. This does not mean that the believer is instantly infused with Christian perfection, but it does mean that the believer does not need to look to anything else to make him spiritually mature (e.g., human philosophy, the Old Testament Mosaic Law, angelic spirits, etc.).

6. a. No. The book of Romans says that believers are under grace (Ro. 6:14) and that Christ is the end of the Law (Ro. 10:4). The Book of Galatians says that the Law was our tutor to bring us to Christ (Gal. 3:19-25). When a person

comes to Christ in salvation, he is no longer under the Law (i.e., the tutor or schoolmaster).

b.   Paul and Barnabas had great dissension and disputation with them. They vehemently disagreed with the Judaizers' position that Christians had to be circumcised and obey the Law of Moses.

c.   Yes. Acts 15:5 specifically says there were some Pharisees who believed (i.e., they were saved), but still believed that Christians must keep the Mosaic Law. The Text also says there was much debate in the Jerusalem church over the issue of the Christians' continuing relationship to the Law (Acts 15:7). This indicated that some in the church believed that Christians had a continuing obligation to keep the Law.

7.   Paul said they had already been spiritually circumcised and that physical circumcision was unnecessary (v. 11). He said the spiritual circumcision did more than remove a small portion of the body - it removed the whole body of sins they had accumulated.

8.   a.   1.   Christ gave life (spiritual) to those who were dead (v. 13).
             2.   Christ forgave all the believers' transgressions (v. 13).
             3.   Christ canceled out the handwriting of ordinances (transgressions) that had accrued to man's account.
             4.   Christ disarmed rulers and authorities (i.e., demonic powers that keep the individual in bondage to Satan, v. 15).

    b.   Answers will vary.

9.   a.   1.   Legalism gives believers a sense of security because they can do specific things that make them feel as if they are pleasing God.
             2.   It is easier to follow a man-made religious system than to "walk in the Spirit" as the Bible commands.
             3.   Legalism produces a certain community (religious) conformity that appeals to man's desires for peer acceptance.
             4.   Other answers could apply.

    b.   Answers will vary.

10. a.   "Let no one judge you."

     b.   Every Christian must learn what the Bible teaches and then learn to stand firmly in the liberty that Christ has given him. This does not mean that believers should flaunt their spiritual liberty in front of other Christians who might stumble (cf. 1 Cor. 8:1-13) but they must come to the place in their spiritual lives where their ultimate goal is to please Christ, not man. A believer cannot stop another Christian from judging him but he can keep his eyes on Christ so that the religious scrutiny of others does not become his spiritual preoccupation.

     c.   A shadow of things to come. Jesus Christ.

11. Answers will vary.

12. The third doctrinal error was mysticism. The Colossian heretics taught that true spiritual advancement could be gained by worshipping angelic beings and submitting to religious self-denial. Mysticism caused its followers to become prideful (vainly puffed up) and to be drawn away from Christ (not holding fast to the Head; i.e., Christ).

13. a. The drawing away of Christians from Christ causes them to be ineffective in their personal ministry to build up other members of the body of Christ.
    b. 1. New Age. 2. Witchcraft. 3. Modern focus on angel worship. 4. Some forms of evangelical Christianity that focus on continuing revelations, visions, and dreams from God (cf. Heb. 1:1).

14. a. The fleshly appetites of the body are a primary cause of sinful conduct and asceticism attempts to control the expression of the sin nature by imposing a rigorous system of self-denial. If an individual could gain mastery over his fleshly temptations he would then be free. While the concept sounds logical, the sinful nature of man cannot be controlled by anything other than by the Spirit of God. The flesh cannot control the flesh regardless of how many restrictions you place on it.
    b. It was ineffective for the believer because it was not able to control the fleshly desires of the sin nature.

15. Answers will vary.

16. It would be wise to point him back to the sufficiency of Christ and the insufficiency of everything else. He should be told that in Christ he is complete because Christ is the fullness of deity in bodily form (Col. 2:9). It would be a good idea to have him read this passage (Col. 2:8-23) carefully to help him understand that Christ is the only answer to true godly living.

Study # 4   **The Renewal Of Christ**

1. a. He should be constantly seeking the things of God.
   b. The believer should center all his spiritual attention around Christ. His attitudes, his action, his life goals, and whole outlook on life should reflect his acknowledgment of Christ's supremacy. The believer's devotion to Christ should take precedence over all earthly allegiances.

2. Although the commands are very similar, there appears to be a slight difference. The Christian is commanded to keep seeking the things which are above where Christ is (v. 1). The Greek verb *"zeteite"* means to seek, desire or strive after by thinking, meditating

or reasoning. The word means a constant searching (Greek present imperative) for those interests that center in Christ. The second command (Gr. *phroneo* - to set your mind on something, to savor) refers more to a settled inner disposition. While the command focuses more on the practical and deliberate choices that a believer makes in life, the second refers to the inner conviction that Christ is the only thing worthy of the believer's continuing devotion. One commentator said, "You must not only seek heaven, you must also think heaven" (Lightfoot).

3. The believer must constantly be thinking how the affairs of everyday living can be administrated from a perspective that acknowledges the supremacy of Christ and brings glory to God. The Christian should neither live for pleasure or self-advancement (the way of the world) nor see his life as part spiritual (i.e., church attendance, Bible reading, etc.) and part secular (i.e., his work, his hobbies, his finances, etc.). The believer must see his vocation as a calling and a commission from God in which he can carry out the work of the Great Commission (cf. Matt. 28:18-20). When a believer adopts this perspective, he begins to see the physical administration of the affairs of life from an eternal point of view, he becomes less frustrated with the minor irritations of living in a fallen world and turns potential frustrations into powerful opportunities for ministry.

4. The believer died with Christ at the time of salvation. A failure to understand this important theological reality is a major cause of spiritual frustration in the Christian life.

5. a. Fornication, uncleanness, passion, evil desire, and covetousness.
  b. Answers will vary.
  c. Idolatry.

6. a. Now.
  b. Anger, wrath, malice, blasphemy, filthy language, and lying.

7. a. Anger (Gr. *orge*) is the characteristic of man's fallen nature that results in various expressions of hostility and indignation. Wrath (Gr. *thumos*) can be translated wrath, fierceness or indignation. It expresses the passion, anger, or heat that boils over and soon subsides. The word is also used of an inflaming wine that drives a drinker to aggressive expressions of passion. Malice (Gr. *kakia*) is an attitude of ill will that one person feels toward another. It often results in secret desires to see misfortune befall another person. Malice covertly rejoices in the misfortunes of others and often mentally plots their demise.
  b. Answers will vary.

8. a. The believer must allow Christ to complete the work that He has begun in the believer at the time of salvation.

b. The phrase "have put on the new man" refers to the new nature that Christ gave the believer at the time of salvation (cf. 2 Cor. 5:17; a new creation). However, the completion of the sanctification process in the life of the believer is a result of the continuing work of God and the continual submission of the believer (Note: the Greek word for "have put on" is a Greek middle participle). The constant renewal of the new nature (cf. "which is renewed") allows the Christian to put off the practices of the old sinful nature and come to a true knowledge or understanding of Christ.

9. When God's people are renewed to a true knowledge of the One who created them, they will be filled with the love of Christ and see people as individual and special creations of God regardless of the color of their skin, their cultural background, or economic status.

10. Answers will vary.

11. a. Answers will vary.
     b. Answers will vary.
     c. Answers will vary.

12. Answers will vary.

13. 1. Believers need to let the peace of God rule in their hearts (v. 15).
     2. They need to minister actively (teaching, counseling, singing, etc.) to fellow believers (v. 16).
     3. They need to do everything from an eternal perspective with a grateful heart (v. 17).

14. 1. "Do not lie to one another" (v. 9).
     2. "Bearing with one another" (v. 13).
     3. "Forgiving one another" (v. 13).
     4. "If anyone has a complaint against another … (v. 13).
     5. "… in all wisdom, teaching and admonishing one another ..." (v. 16).
     6. Other answers could include: "Put on tender mercies ..." (v. 12).

Study # 5   The New Self In Christ

1. a. She can be subject to her husband (Col. 3:18).
    b. He can love his wife and not be embittered against her.
    c. They can be obedient to their parents.

2. a. 1. The command is stated clearly in Scripture (v. 18). It is a dangerous thing to simply eliminate a biblical command on cultural grounds. If this perspective is used without legitimate biblical basis, essentially every command in Scripture could be eliminated.
        2. The male headship of the family in some ways reflects the administrative order of the Godhead. The submission of the wife models the administrative subordination of Jesus Christ to God the Father. It is important to realize that, in both situations (husband - wife; God the Father - Jesus Christ the Son), subordination does not mean inferiority.
    b. 1. The wife's obedience is voluntary.
        2. The wife's obedience is limited to her husband's authority. The Bible does not teach male superiority over women in general.
        3. The wife's obedience is restricted to the parameters of Scripture. She is not obligated to follow her husband if his demands directly conflict with the specific spiritual commands (cf. Acts 5:29). However, if she must defer to the authority of the Bible rather than obey her husband, she must continue to demonstrate an attitude of humility and respect.

3. The biblical teaching emphasizes individual responsibility within the marriage union rather than the rights of the individual partners. This does not mean that there are no implied rights within marriage. It does mean that the marriage partners should focus on their individual responsibilities rather than what their spouse is or is not doing within the marriage.

4. Fathers (and mothers, cf. Pro. 1:8, 6:20) should not place unrealistic demands and expectations on their children. They must avoid all that will irritate or exasperate their children - injustice, unreasonable punishment, constant faultfinding, unfair comparison with other children, ridicule, etc. The father (and mother) should attempt to understand the natural emotional development of the child. They should strive to live for God in all aspects of life and confront all hypocrisy in their own lives - a major cause of teenage rebellion and anger. Other answers could apply.

5. a. 1. "Not with eyeservice, as men-pleasers" (v. 22).
        2. "But in sincerity of heart" (v. 22).
        3. "Fearing God" (v. 22).
        4. "And whatever you do, do it heartily, as to the Lord, and not to men" (v. 23).
    b. Yes. Many servants or slaves in the ancient Roman empire experienced a great degree of freedom in the relationship with their masters. Although our modern concept of a slave reminds us of shackles and chains, many slaves held social positions of political and economic significance. For this reason, it is correct to apply the slave-master relationship to the modern employee -employer relationship.

6. "As to the Lord" or "you serve the Lord Christ."

7. If God's people do not fulfill their work responsibilities, they will reap the consequences of their error (e.g., termination, demotion, probation, etc.). They cannot expect God to supernaturally protect them if they are insubordinate, slothful, etc. ("and there is no partiality").

8. The Christian employer must constantly remind himself (herself) that he has another Authority to whom he must ultimately answer. If the Christian employer can remember this (cf. "knowing"), he will be motivated to treat his employees with justice and fairness.

9. The Greek word for continue means holding something with strength, not neglecting or letting it drop. The early Christians continued or devoted themselves (cf. Acts 2:42, same Greek word) to the apostles' teaching and to fellowship, to the breaking of bread and to prayer. Christians should not neglect prayer, both corporate and private. The phrase "watch in the same" means never neglecting or growing weary or careless. Believers should never allow prayer to become a careless ritual. They should be diligent in prayer to God for themselves and others (cf. Eph. 6:18). The third phrase "with thanksgiving" means that, as believers pray, they should express their appreciation for what God has done and the confidence for what He will do in the future.

10. a. Paul asked the Colossians to join him in prayer so that God would providentially open a free opportunity for the ministry of the gospel. The mystery is the whole blessed gospel message of God's universal redemption that is made available through Jesus Christ's work on the cross. Paul desired to make this magnificent truth clear to all who would listen (v. 4).
    b. Answers will vary.

11. Paul exhorted the Colossian Christians to exercise wisdom in their daily contact with non-Christians. This would help eliminate and hindrances to the gospel message and help them accept the truth of eternal salvation. Paul did not see contact with the world as a threat, but as an opportunity to demonstrate the love of God to lost humanity.

12. Paul said Tychicus was his beloved brother, a faithful minister and a fellowservant in the Lord (v. 7). He said Onesimus was his faithful and beloved brother (v. 9).

13. 1. Priscilla (Ro. 16:3). 2. Aquila (Ro. 16:3). 3. Epaphroditus (Ph. 2:25-30).

14. a. 1. He labored (Gr. *agonizomenos*, 1:29) in prayer for them so that they would come to spiritual maturity (i.e., stand firm and fully assured in all the will of God).
        2. He had a deep concern for the believers of the region that he obviously shared with Paul.

3. He sought spiritual help from the apostle Paul to correct the doctrinal problem that had developed in the church.

b. Paul wanted Archippus to pay close attention to the ministry God had given him (i.e., the church) so that he might fulfill the work God had given him.

c. He asked the church to remember his imprisonment. This likely meant that they were to continue to pray for his release.

15. The book of Colossians teaches the supremacy of Christ over all creation.

16. 1. Humanistic philosophy. 2. Legalism. 3. Mysticism. 4. Asceticism.

17. Answers will vary.

The Final Exam

Every person will eventually stand before God in judgment – the final exam. The Bible says, *"And as it is appointed unto men once to die, but after this the judgment"* (Heb. 9:27).

May I ask you a question? *"If you died today, do you know for certain that you would go to heaven?"* I did not ask you if you are religious or if you are a church member; nor did I ask you if you have had some encounter with God - a meaningful, spiritual experience. I did not even ask you if you believe in God, angels, or if you are trying to live a good life. The question I am asking you is this: *"If you died today, do you know for certain that you would go to heaven?"*

When you die, you will stand alone before God in judgment. You will either be saved for all eternity or you will be separated from God for all eternity in what the Bible calls the lake of fire (Ro. 14:12; Rev. 20:11-15). Tragically, many religious people who believe in God are not going to be accepted by Him when they die.

> *"Many will say to Me in that day, `Lord, Lord, have we not prophesied in Your name, cast out demons in Your name, and done many wonders in Your name?' And then I will declare to them, `I never knew you. Depart from Me, you who practice lawlessness!'"* (Matt 7:22, 23).

God loves you and wants you to go to heaven (Jn. 3:16; 2 Pet. 3:9). If you are not sure where you will spend eternity, you are not prepared to meet God. God wants you to know for certain that you will go to heaven.

> *"... behold, now is the accepted time, behold now is the day of salvation."* (2 Cor. 6:2).

The words **"behold"** and **"now"** are repeated because God wants you to know that you can be saved today. You do not need to hear those terrible words, *"Depart from Me...".* Isn't that great news?

Jesus Himself said, *"You must be born again"* (Jn. 3:7). These are not the words of a pastor, a church or a particular denomination. They are the words of Jesus Christ Himself. You <u>must</u> be born again (saved from eternal damnation) before you die; otherwise, it will be too late when you die! You can know for certain today that God will accept you into heaven when you die.

> *"These things I have written to you who believe in the name of the Son of God that you may <u>know</u> that you have eternal life ..."* (1 Jn. 5:13).

The phrase, *"... you may know"* means that you can know for certain before you die that you will go to heaven. To be born again, you must understand and believe (this means to place your faith in) four essential spiritual truths. These truths are right from the Bible so you know you can trust them – they are not some man-made religious traditions. Now let's consider these four essential spiritual truths.

1St Essential Spiritual Truth. <u>The Bible teaches that you are a sinner and separated from God.</u>

No one is righteous in God's eyes, including you. To be righteous means to be totally without any sin, even a single act.

"There is none righteous, no, not one; There is none who understands; There is none who seeks after God. They have all turned aside; They have together become unprofitable. There is none who does good, no, not one." (Ro. 3:10-12).

"for all have sinned and fall short of the glory of God" (Ro. 3:23).

Look at the words God uses to show that all men are sinners – "**none, not one, all turned aside, no, not one**". God is making a point – all men are sinners, including you. No man is good (perfectly without sin) in His sight. The reason is sin.

Have you ever lied, lusted, hated someone, stolen anything or taken God's name in vain, even once? These are all sins. Only one sin makes you a sinner and unrighteous in God's eyes.

Are you willing to admit to God that you are a sinner? If you are, then tell Him right now you have sinned. You can say the words in your heart or out loud - it doesn't matter, but be honest with God. Now check the box if you have just admitted you are a sinner.

❑   *God, I admit I am a sinner in your eyes.*

Now, let's look at the second essential spiritual truth.

2nd Essential Spiritual Truth. <u>The Bible teaches that you cannot save yourself or earn your way to heaven.</u>

Man's sin is a very serious problem in the eyes of God. Your sin separates you from God, both now and for all eternity unless you are born again.

"For the wages of sin is death ..." (Romans 6:23).

"And you He made alive, who were dead in trespasses and sins," (Eph. 2:1).

Wages are a payment that are earned by a person for what he or she has done.   Your sin has earned you the wages of death that means separation from God. If you die without ever having been born again, you will be separated from God after death.

You cannot save yourself or purchase your entrance into heaven.   The Bible says that man is, *"... not redeemed with corruptible things, like gold or silver ..."* (1 Pet. 1:18). If you owned all the money in the world, you could not buy your entrance into heaven nor can you buy your way into heaven with good works.

"For by grace are you have been saved through faith; and that <u>not of yourselves: it is the gift of God, <u>not of works, lest any man should boast</u></u>" (Eph. 2:8, 9).

The Bible says salvation is, *"not of yourselves", "... not of works, lest any man should boast."* Salvation from eternal judgment cannot be earned by doing good works – it is a gift of God. There is nothing you can do to purchase your way into heaven because you are already unrighteous in God's eyes.

If you understand you cannot save yourself, then tell God right now that you are a sinner, separated from Him and you cannot save yourself. Check the box below if you have just done that.

❑ *God, I admit that I am separated from You because of my sin. I realize that I cannot save myself.*

Now let's look at the third essential spiritual truth.

3rd Essential Spiritual Truth. <u>The Bible teaches that Jesus Christ died on the cross to pay the complete penalty for your sin and to purchase a place in heaven for you.</u>

Jesus Christ, the sinless Son of God, lived a perfect life, died on the cross and rose from the dead to pay the penalty for your sin and purchase a place in heaven for you. He died on the cross on your behalf, in your place, as your substitute, so you do not have to go to hell. Jesus Christ is the only acceptable substitute for your sin.

"For He (God, the Father) made Him (Jesus) who knew (committed) no sin to be sin for us that we might become the righteousness of God in Him" (2 Cor. 5:21).

"I (Jesus) am the way, the truth, and the life. No one comes to the Father except through me" (Jn. 14:6).

"Nor is there salvation in any other, for there is no other name under heaven given among men by which we must be saved." (Acts 4:12).

Jesus Christ is your only hope and means of salvation. Because you are a sinner, you cannot pay for your sins, but Jesus paid the penalty for your sins by dying on the cross in your place. Friend, there is salvation in no one else – not angels, not some religious leader, not even your religious good works. No religious act such as baptism, confirmation or joining a church can save you. There is no other way, no other name who can save you. Only Jesus Christ can save you. You must be saved by accepting Jesus Christ's substitutionary sacrifice for your sins or you will be lost forever.

Do you see clearly that Jesus Christ is the only way to God in heaven? If you understand this truth, tell God that you understand and check the box below.

❑ *God, I understand that Jesus Christ died to pay the penalty for my sin. I understand that His death on the cross is the only acceptable sacrifice for my sin.*

4th Essential Spiritual Truth. <u>By faith, you must trust in Jesus Christ alone for eternal life and call upon Him to be your Savior and Lord.</u>

Many religious people admit they have sinned. They believe Jesus Christ died for the sins of the world but they are not saved. Why? Thousands of moral, religious people have never completely placed their faith in Jesus Christ <u>alone</u> for eternal life. They think they must believe in Jesus Christ as a real person and do good works to earn their way to heaven. They are not trusting Jesus Christ alone.   To be saved, you must trust in Jesus Christ <u>alone</u> for eternal life. Look what the Bible teaches about trusting Jesus Christ alone for salvation.

> *"that if you confess with your mouth the Lord Jesus and believe in your heart that God has raised Him from the dead, <u>you will be saved</u>. For with the heart one believes unto righteousness, and with the mouth confession is made unto salvation. For there is no distinction between Jew or Greek, for the same Lord over all <u>is rich to all</u> who call upon Him. For <u>whoever calls on the name of the Lord shall be saved</u>" (Ro. 10:9, 10, 12, 13).*

Do you see what God is saying? To be saved or born again, you need to trust Jesus Christ <u>alone </u>for eternal life. Jesus Christ paid for your complete salvation. Jesus said, *"It is finished"* (Jn. 19:30). Jesus paid for your salvation completely when He shed His blood on the cross for your sin.

If you believe that God resurrected Jesus Christ (proving God's acceptance of Jesus as a worthy sacrifice for man's sin) and you are willing to confess the Lord Jesus Christ as your Savior and Lord (lord, master of your life), you will be saved.

Friend, right now God is offering you the greatest gift in the world. God wants to give you the <u>gift</u> of eternal life, the <u>gift </u>of His complete forgiveness for all your sins, and the <u>gift</u> of His unconditional acceptance into heaven when you die. Will you accept His free gift now, right where you are?

Are you unsure how to receive the gift of eternal life? Let me help you. Do you remember that I said you needed to understand and accept four essential spiritual truths. First, you admitted you are a sinner. Second, you admitted you were separated from God because of your sin and you could not save yourself. Third, you realized that Jesus Christ was the only way to heaven – no other name could save you.

Now, you must call upon the Lord Jesus Christ once and for all to save your lost soul. Ask Him right now to save you. Just take God at His word – He will not lie to you! This is the kind of simple faith you need to be saved. If you are still uncertain what to do, pray this prayer to God. Remember, the words must come from your heart.

> *God, I am a sinner and deserve to go to hell. Thank you Jesus for dying on the cross for me and for purchasing a place in heaven for me. Please forgive me for all my sins and take me to heaven when I die. I call on you Jesus right now to save me forever. Thank you for saving me now. Amen.*

If you just asked Jesus Christ to save you in the best way you know how, God just saved you. He said in His Holy Word, ***"Whoever calls upon the name of the Lord shall be saved" (Ro. 10:13)*** and the **whoever** includes you - it is that simple. God just gave you the gift of eternal life by faith. You have just been born again according to the Bible.

You will not come into eternal judgment and you will not perish in the lake of fire – you are saved forever! Read this verse over carefully and let it sink into your heart.

>***"Most assuredly, I say to you, he who hears My word and believes in Him who sent Me has everlasting life, and shall not come into judgment, but has passed from death into life." (Jn. 5:24)***

Now let me ask you a couple more questions. According to God's Holy Word (Jn. 5:24), not your feelings, what kind of life did God just give you? _____. What two words did God say at the beginning of the verse to assure you that He is not lying to you? _____ _____ . Are you going to come into judgment - YES or NO? Have you passed from spiritual death into life - YES or NO?

Friend, you have just been born again. You just became a child of God. We would like to help you grow in your new Christian life. We will send you a Spiritual Birth Certificate to remind you of your spiritual birthday and some Bible study materials to help you understand more about the Christian life. To receive these helpful materials free of charge, photocopy the form below, fill it out and send it to us by mail or you can e-mail us at resources @LamplightersUSA.org.

Lamplighters Response Card

❑ I just accepted Jesus Christ as my Savior and Lord on (date) _____, 200____ at _____.

❑ Please send me the Spiritual Birth Certificate and the Bible Study materials to help me grow as a Christian.

❑ I would like to begin attending a Bible-believing church in the area where I live. Please recommend some Bible-believing churches in the area where I live.

❑ I already know of a good Bible-believing church that I will be attending to help me grow as a new Christian.

Name _____

Address _____

City _____ State _____ Zip _____

Email address _____

Lamplighters International, P.O. Box 44725, Eden Prairie, Minnesota 55344

To order additional Lamplighters discipleship materials, contact your local Christian bookstore or call Lamplighters International at 1-800 507-9516 (toll-free ordering). You can also write us at PO Box 44725, Eden Prairie, Minnesota, 55344 or order online at www.LamplightersUSA.org.